What Makes Day and Night

This Is a Let's-Read-and-Find-Out Science Book®

Revised Edition

What Makes Day and Night

Franklyn M. Branley · illustrated by Arthur Dorros

HarperCollins*Publishers*

Other Recent Let's-Read-and-Find-Out Science Books® You Will Enjoy

Air Is All Around You • Ant Cities • Baby Whales Drink Milk • Be a Friend to Trees • The Beginning of the Earth • The Big Dipper • Comets • Danger—Icebergs! • Digging Up Dinosaurs • Dinosaur Bones • Dinosaurs Are Different • A Drop of Blood • Ducks Don't Get Wet • Ears Are For Hearing • Earthquakes • Eclipse: Darkness in Daytime • Evolution • Feel the Wind • Fireflies in the Night • Flash, Crash, Rumble, and Roll • Follow the Water from Brook to Ocean • Fossils Tell of Long Ago • Germs Make Me Sick! • Get Ready for Robots! • Glaciers • Gravity Is a Mystery • How a Seed Grows • How Do Apples Grow? • How Many Teeth? • How We Learned the Earth Is Round • How You Talk • Hurricane Watch • I'm Growing! • Is There Life in Outer Space? • Journey into a Black Hole • Look at Your Eyes • Look Out for Turtles! • Milk From Cow to Carton • The Moon Seems to Change • My Feet • My Five Senses • My Hands • My Visit to the Dinosaurs • An Octopus Is Amazing • The Planets in Our Solar System • Rock Collecting • Rockets and Satellites • Shooting Stars • The Skeleton Inside You • Snakes Are Hunters • Snow Is Falling • The Sun: Our Nearest Star • Sunshine Makes the Seasons • Switch On, Switch Off • Tornado Alert • Volcanoes • What Happened to the Dinosaurs? • What Happens to a Hamburger • What Makes a Shadow? • What Makes Day and Night • What the Moon Is Like • What Will the Weather Be? • Where Does the Garbage Go? • Your Skin and Mine

The *Let's-Read-and-Find-Out Science Book* series was originated by Dr. Franklyn M. Branley, Astronomer Emeritus and former Chairman of the American Museum–Hayden Planetarium, and was formerly co-edited by him and Dr. Roma Gans, Professor Emeritus of Childhood Education, Teachers College, Columbia University. For a complete catalog of Let's-Read-and-Find-Out Science Books, write to HarperCollins Children's Books, 10 East 53rd Street, New York, NY 10022.

What Makes Day and Night
Text copyright © 1961, 1986 by Franklyn M. Branley
Illustration copyright © 1986 by Arthur Dorros
Printed in Mexico   For information address HarperCollins Children's Books, a division of HarperCollins Publishers, 10 East 53rd Street, New York, NY 10022.
3 4 5 6 7 8 9 10
Revised Edition

Library of Congress Cataloging-in-Publication Data
Branley, Franklyn Mansfield, 1915–
    What makes day and night.
    (Let's-read-and-find-out science book)
    Summary: A simple explanation of how the rotation of the earth causes night and day.
    1. Earth—Rotation—Juvenile literature.
2. Day—Juvenile literature. 3. Night—Juvenile literature. [1. Earth—Rotation.
2. Day. 3. Night]
I. Dorros, Arthur, ill. II. Title. III. Series
QB633.B73 1986   525'.35   85-47903
ISBN 0-690-04523-9
ISBN 0-690-04524-7 (lib. bdg.)

What Makes Day and Night

We all live on the earth.

The earth is our planet.
It is round like a big ball.
And it is spinning.

It's hard to believe the earth is always turning, because we don't feel any motion. This is because the earth spins smoothly—always at the same speed.

SUN   EARTH

This is a photograph of the earth. It was taken by a camera aboard the Apollo 17 spacecraft. You can see that the earth is round.

If you were way out in space and watching the earth, you would see it spin. The earth spins around once in twenty-four hours.

Light from the sun falls on one-half of the spinning earth. The half in the light has day. The other half is dark. It is in the earth's shadow. That half has night.

As the earth spins we move through the light, into the darkness, and back again. We have day and night.

Imagine you are in a spaceship high above the North Pole. Imagine you can stay there twenty-four hours and watch the earth make one complete turn.

North Pole

South Pole

As the earth turns we have sunrise, daylight, sunset, and night.

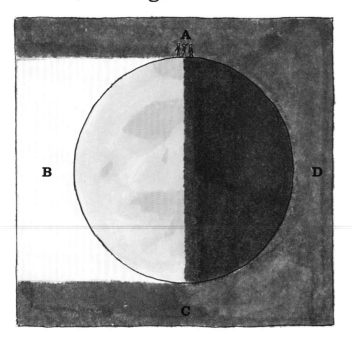

People at A have sunrise.

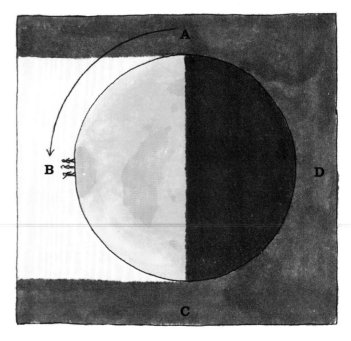

Later, because the earth is turning, they are at B. It is the middle of the day for them. It is noontime.

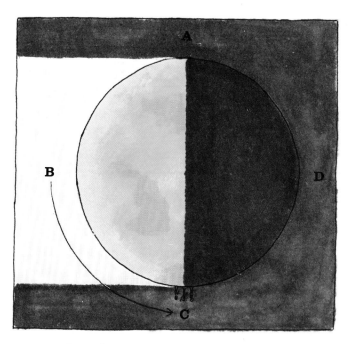

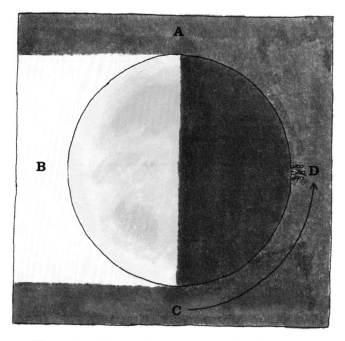

As the earth turns, it carries them to C. They have sunset.

By the time they reach D it is the middle of the night for them. It is midnight. At the end of twenty-four hours they have sunrise again.

You can see how we move from daylight to darkness by doing an experiment. You will be the earth, and a lamp will be the sun.

sunrise

day

Stand so that your left side is toward the lamp. Hold your arms out all the way. Your left hand points toward the lamp.

This is sunrise.

Stay in the same spot. Keep your arms out from your sides, and turn to your left. Now the lamp is in front of you. It is the middle of the day. It is noontime.

sunset

night

Keep turning until your right hand points toward the lamp. You are turning away from the light. It is sunset.

Keep turning until your back is toward the lamp. It is night. But your back is in daylight. Half of you is always light, and half is dark. It's the same with the earth.

The earth is always turning. It never stops. Round and round it goes. And it goes very fast. About 1000 miles an hour. As the earth turns we are always moving from day to night. And from night to day.

You can see this happen. If you are awake very early, you can see sunrise. The earth is moving you toward the sun.

The earth keeps turning. Later in the day we begin to turn away from the sun. You can see sunset.

About twenty-four hours after sunrise, the sun will rise again. It all happens because the earth is spinning around.

As the earth turns, the sun seems to move across the sky.

If you were on the moon, you would also have day and night. But the moon spins very slowly, so days and nights are long. Places on the moon have two weeks of daylight and then two weeks of darkness.

During one night on the moon the earth spins around fourteen times.

The turning earth gives us about twelve hours of daylight and twelve hours of darkness. That seems just about right for all of us on the planet earth.

Franklyn M. Branley, Astronomer Emeritus and former chairman of the American Museum-Hayden Planetarium, is well-known as the author of many popular and award-winning books about astronomy and other sciences for young people of all ages. He is the originator of the Let's-Read-and-Find-Out Science series.

Dr. Branley holds degrees from New York University, Columbia University, and the State University of New York at New Paltz.

He and his wife live in Sag Harbor, New York.

Arthur Dorros is the illustrator of CHARLIE'S HOUSE and combined author and illustrator of PRETZELS AND ALLIGATOR SHOES. Educated at the University of Wisconsin and Pacific Oaks College, he has been a participant in the Artist-in-Residence Program in New York City, where he taught writing and book illustration to children. An avid traveler, Mr. Dorros now lives in Seattle, Washington.